Successful
People Skills
In A Week

Christine Harvey

The Teach Yourself series h~~ ~   ·sted around the world

~ek' business books is

around the world to

hat the experts learn

Christine Harvey and her organization have trained thousands of people across Europe, America and Asia – from the British and Australian Institutes of Management to the US Military – in the seven effective methods to improve people skills you'll discover here. She is frequently interviewed on radio and TV. She is the author of six books, including *Successful People Skills in a Week*, *Successful Selling in a Week*, *Your Pursuit of Profit*, *Public Speaking & Leadership Building*, *Can a Girl Run for President?* and *Secrets of the World's Top Sales Performers*. Few authors have such worldwide acceptance: her books are published in 28 languages.

Successful People Skills

Christine Harvey

www.inaweek.co.uk

Teach® Yourself

Hodder Education

338 Euston Road, London NW1 3BH.

Hodder Education is an Hachette UK company

First published in UK 1992 by Hodder Education

First published in US 2012 by The McGraw-Hill Companies, Inc.

This edition published 2012.

Previous editions of this book were published by Hodder in 1992 and 1998.

British Library Cataloguing in Publication Data: a catalogue record for this title is available from the British Library.

Library of Congress Catalog Card Number: on file.

10 9 8 7 6 5 4 3

The publisher has used its best endeavours to ensure that any website addresses referred to in this book are correct and active at the time of going to press. However, the publisher and the author have no responsibility for the websites and can make no guarantee that a site will remain live or that the content will remain relevant, decent or appropriate.

The publisher has made every effort to mark as such all words which it believes to be trademarks. The publisher should also like to make it clear that the presence of a word in the book, whether marked or unmarked, in no way affects its legal status as a trademark.

Every reasonable effort has been made by the publisher to trace the copyright holders of material in this book. Any errors or omissions should be notified in writing to the publisher, who will endeavour to rectify the situation for any reprints and future editions.

Hachette UK's policy is to use papers that are natural, renewable and recyclable products and made from wood grown in sustainable forests. The logging and manufacturing processes are expected to conform to the environmental regulations of the country of origin.

www.hoddereducation.co.uk

Typeset by Cenveo Publisher Services.

Printed and bound by CPI Group (UK) Ltd, Croydon, CR0 4YY.

Also available in ebook

Contents

Introduction

People skills are not something we are taught in school, and neither is the subject of motivation or raising performance levels. And yet do you know anyone who doesn't want to motivate or raise performance levels in themselves, their employees and even their children? Probably not!

This book covers a week when each of the seven days focuses on a different aspect of people skills. Some of you will be keen to try each one, while others will find a specific need – maybe for use with an employee, a son or daughter, a spouse or even yourself – and focus on that, then move on to another need and fulfil that.

One thing you can be certain of is that each principle and each process really does work. Participants in our seminars have had immediate results, regardless of their industry or culture. Whether they are in Asia, Europe or America, their results have been exceptional.

People skills are a commodity everyone wants more of. We need them on a daily basis to run our lives, to help others, to lead people and to reach our goals. The ability to work with, lead and motivate ourselves and others affects our success in business and our satisfaction in life. By using a few practical methods, we can improve our results enormously.

People skills, particularly in the area of motivation and performance, can be the most rewarding of skills. They are achievable by everyone. There is no limit to the situations in which they can be applied, or to the level of expertise you can reach.

As an author, one of the greatest pleasures I've had is to update this book, thus bringing more insight to you, the reader. As I've re-examined each chapter, I'm reminded of hundreds of stories from people around the world who have used these methods and developed skills to change their world. For example, I've known a business owner who rescued his most important employee who was on the verge of quitting, a woman who reunited with her best friend after an argument many years earlier, and a man who realized he was undermining rather than supporting his spouse.

Whether you are reading this because there is someone you want to motivate or whose performance you want to improve, or because you want to enhance your own leadership skills, using the techniques in this book will help you achieve your goals. So dig in and enjoy. I wish you success in your journey, every step of the way.

It would be my great pleasure to hear how you applied the material. Writing a book is like giving birth to an offspring, taking about nine months to develop after years of personal growth. As our children grow to be teens and adults, it's nice to hear great stories about them. So, if you have questions or stories to tell me – or you wish to enquire about our seminars – you can reach me at ChristineHarvey@ChristineHarvey.com, or via the publishers. Enjoy!

Christine Harvey

SUNDAY

Raise morale – raise performance

We all know that, when morale is high, be it in yourself or your organization, it seems that anything is possible. When morale is low, the opposite is true. Performance is likely to be low, and life may seem bleak.

Some people think that attitude is difficult to change, and yet research shows that attitude is 10 per cent determined by outside forces and 90 per cent by our own minds. If this is true, why then is our attitude to life so often different from what we want it to be?

Part of the reason is that we model our attitude from people around us at such an early age that we don't ask ourselves if that's the attitude we want for life. We struggle with it, because somehow it doesn't fit us: it fits like someone else's shoes.

How do we go about improving morale? Today you'll examine three pillars of people skills with regard to motivation and morale. These are positivity, gratitude and self-worth. A unique combination, you might think, and they all reflect a certain attitude: is our glass half empty or half full?

The attitudes that motivate

If the shoes don't fit, what shoes would fit better? If we look at the most motivated people, we find that they have three attitudes that guide their life perspective. These are:

- positivity
- gratitude
- self-worth.

Positivity

Imagine for the moment that you are standing at the edge of a pond, and that in your hands you hold two pebbles.

In your left hand you have a pollution pebble and, if you throw it into the pond, it will pollute the water for generations to come. In your right hand you hold a purification pebble and, if you throw that one into the pond, it will purify the water for generations to come. The choice of which pebble to throw is yours.

Now imagine that the words we use are like the pebbles and the people in our lives are like the water. If we choose negative words, they pollute our mind and destroy motivation – our own, other people's and, perhaps, that of generations to come. If we choose positive words, on the other hand, we purify, we support and we motivate.

What kind of environment can you create with your words, for yourself and for the people in your life?

Don't pollute your motivation
Can you afford to be gentler with yourself, less hard on yourself? People often have wonderful achievements and talents and yet they choose to belittle themselves by focusing on what they didn't achieve or can't do. Is this honouring the true potential we have within us? Is this purifying or polluting our motivation?

The ripple effect

A man once came up to me after a speech I made and said, 'I'm going home with a completely new approach to my son. He's been trying to start a business and I've been telling him everything I thought he was doing wrong. I thought I was helping. Now I'm going to point out all the positive things he's doing and build up his faith.'

He realized that the ripple effect, like the pebble in the water, would carry his motivation from person to person and back again into their relationship.

Can you afford to be more positive with other people? Think about your own life. Who is waiting for you to motivate them? Think of your career. Think of your family. Think also of your associations. What can you say to people in order to let them see their successes – to keep them going?

7

We do it automatically with children. When they learn to walk, we cheer them on. We clap and give them words of encouragement. We don't wait until they fall down and then say, 'Stupid!' Yet that's often what happens in business and the community. We criticize people the minute something goes wrong, but we forget to give them positive reinforcement to keep them going.

> **'Don't criticize others for the way things are being done unless you're prepared to volunteer to do them yourself.'**
> Plaque at the registration table of a social club

No wonder we don't get as much support from members of our community or our employees as we would like, and that often we lose them altogether. The minute they do something, they expect someone to criticize them. And very little of this criticism is ever balanced with positive feedback. And yet we could get better results if we gave positive reinforcement.

 Start to think of yourself as a motivator. Realize that you may be the only one in another person's life who is able to give positive reinforcement.

Be conscious of your power
Think again of those purification and pollution pebbles. What can you commit to doing to purify the waters of the mind – your mind and the minds of others?

Gratitude

> **'Two men looked out through prison bars.
> One saw the mud, the other the stars.'**
>
> Dale Carnegie

We have the power to see the best or the worst of every situation. The mud and the stars are both there. We can choose what to focus on. When we focus on the mud, we feel bogged down. When we focus on the stars, we feel hope and gratitude.

If we think for a moment of the world around us, we realize how much we have to be grateful for. In the 1990s, millions of people became free of the Communist system. For them, despite the economic struggles, the pleasures of freedom and openness in society were marvellous. These are pleasures we in the West took for granted.

Each time I travel to and from countries in the developing world, I experience culture shock in each direction. On entering, I realize that these are people who have so little of the luxury we take for granted in the developed world. When I return again to my own environment, I have the feeling of imbalance for having so much which we seldom appreciate: well-paved roads, good health care, a reliable electricity supply, goods in the shops.

Above all these things that we have to be grateful for, however, is the sheer marvel of our creation, the power of our brain to create, of our heart and our soul to love and to feel. And yet how much do we value them? We're not even behind prison bars, and yet we don't let ourselves see the stars.

When we focus on gratitude, there's no room for negativity. When we focus on gratitude, motivation automatically comes through. Gratitude, in fact, blocks out negativity.

Gratitude, like positivity, is contagious and magnetic. If we want to motivate others, let's start with ourselves, then go forward.

Self-worth

It's easy to see how self-worth is important to our own motivation, but let's look first at how important it is in motivating other people at work and in the community. If you want more co-operation from the people around you, think about using self-worth as a motivator, as in the following case study.

People need to feel wanted and cared about. Their self-worth is important and it's up to us to enhance it. When each person's self-worth is high, the group's morale is high. When the group's morale is high, the group flourishes.

Self-worth transference to organizations

Have you ever stopped to listen to some people talking about their company? It sometimes seems that they can find nothing good to say about it. Yet the company might have a 50-year history of serving the community and be recognized for good quality.

Why should this be so? If a person's feeling of self-worth is low, they transpose that image on to their organization. We should consider it our responsibility to help them see the best in themselves. Gradually, as their self-esteem goes up, they'll begin to see the best in their company.

Self-worth acknowledgement for yourself

One secondary school teacher in America gave his students the assignment of writing an autobiography. Included in it, he told them, must be a statement about the student's strengths and talents.

Using self-worth as a motivator

Two executives in London were faced with the fact that membership of their service club was flagging. They had to do something quickly or it would face collapse. They planned their strategy for gaining new members and decided to put their first focus on giving attention to their current members.

Here's what they did. They put a table at the door of the meeting room with two of their most friendly committee members. Then they greeted each member as they entered, and poured them a glass of wine. Next, they got them engaged in conversation with another member. In other words, they showed them that they mattered.

They also sent out a newsletter a few days before each meeting announcing the speaker. They had a telephone committee who called each member personally three days before the meeting to say they looked forward to seeing them. Notice they said 'looked forward to seeing them'. That's different from pressuring them or making them feel guilty; it's making them feel important.

Attendance by members shot up immediately. And they kept coming. They brought friends. The membership grew just by taking care of the old members.

Upon getting this assignment, most of the students were dumbfounded. No one could say anything good about themselves. It didn't seem right to them.

Finally, one of the students went to the teacher to admit his dilemma. This is what he reports hearing the teacher say.

'You know Terry, the problem with our upbringing is that we're taught to be so modest that we don't even see the value in ourselves. It doesn't help us to serve the purpose we were put here for. It doesn't help us fulfil the reasons for our existence.'

Terry was only 14 when he had that experience, and the impact was great. He developed an attitude he uses in management today. The attitude is this:

'It's all right to honour our own humanity and to honour the humanity of others. It's all right to honour our organization and all that we work for. It's all right for all of us to help others to learn that too.'

Motivation and morale

What realization do we come to about motivation from people who succeed best as motivators?

1 We must be **positive**, not negative. When we are positive, we draw people to us like a magnet. When we are positive with other people, we feel good about ourselves.

2 We must have **gratitude**. When we do, we project harmony, which is rare and attractive in group dynamics. It draws the best people to us.
3 We should never underestimate the importance of **self-worth**, for without it we cannot fulfil our potential.

Each of us has phenomenal ability. Each of us has been given phenomenal talent. When it comes to motivation, it's easy to think that our life can change from gaining new information. But is information or knowledge alone enough?

Will it do us any good, for example, to know that people need positive words of encouragement from us, if we don't provide them? Is it enough to understand that we can affect the self-esteem of others, if we don't *do* it?

No. Knowledge without action creates no change. It's like standing at the edge of the pond with those purification pebbles in your hand but not using them. It's having the power, but not using it. It does no good for anyone.

People skills in action

Use an actions table like the one below to enhance your own techniques and achievements. Ideas for development include the following.

1 Examine the words you use in speaking and writing. What percentage is negative and what percentage is positive?
2 Do you belittle yourself unnecessarily?

3 Do you criticize people with your comments, jokes or questions?
4 Remind yourself regularly of the power of your words and thoughts.
5 Does gratitude play a large enough part in your life?
6 Is your self-worth high enough? If not, list your strengths and stop thinking about your weaknesses.
7 Complete other points as they relate to you, according to your needs.

Create your answers

- Of the above ideas, which one is likely to yield the best results for you?
- What percentage performance increase could you realistically expect?
- How long would it take:
  - to develop the idea?
  - to get results?
- Who would have to be involved?
- What date should you start?
- What is the first step you should take?

Think carefully of the impact of your positivity, your gratitude and your self-worth on yourself and on the people in your life. Take today to decide what specific actions you will take, and note them down in a table like the one below.

Actions I will take

Positivity	
Gratitude	
Self-worth	

Summary

Today we looked at three pillars of people skills with regard to motivation: positivity, gratitude and the fostering of self-worth.

We learned that positivity can purify rather than pollute our motivation, supporting it rather than dissipating it. We examined the power of words, and how our words can have ripple effects on ourselves and others for generations to come.

With regard to gratitude, we saw that we have the power to see the best or the worst in every situation like the men looking through prison bars: one saw the mud, the other saw the stars. We can choose to see the stars by being grateful for all that we have, and yet we often deny ourselves of that joy, focusing instead on the cup half empty.

With regard to self-worth, we saw that often we've been taught to be so modest that we don't see the true value in ourselves. We learned that it's all right to honour our humanity and the humanity of others.

Finally, we learned that by focusing on three pillars of motivational people skills – positivity, gratitude and self-worth – we allow our phenomenal abilities to unfold.

SUNDAY

MONDAY

TUESDAY

WEDNESDAY

THURSDAY

FRIDAY

SATURDAY

Fact-check (answers at the back)

1. What guides the life perspective of the most motivated people?
a) Positivity ☐
b) Gratitude ☐
c) Self-worth ☐
d) All of the above ☐

2. When trying to motivate other people, what should you do?
a) Tell them everything they are doing wrong to save them heartache ☐
b) Say nothing for fear of demotivating them ☐
c) Point out all the positive things they are doing, to build up their faith ☐
d) None of the above ☐

3. When we choose positive words, what effect do we have on people?
a) We purify rather than pollute the environment ☐
b) We support them ☐
c) We motivate them ☐
d) All of the above ☐

4. Who is likely to be waiting for you to motivate them?
a) Your family ☐
b) Your associates ☐
c) Members of your community ☐
d) All of the above ☐

5. When we focus on gratitude, what is there no room for?
a) Negativity ☐
b) Hearsay ☐
c) Gossip ☐
d) All of the above ☐

6. What do we need to help people feel?
a) Happy as often as possible ☐
b) Wanted and cared about ☐
c) Challenged ☐
d) None of the above ☐

7. What causes us to be so modest that we don't see our true value?
a) Society ☐
b) Television ☐
c) Our upbringing ☐
d) Self-image ☐

8. What happens when we are positive?
a) We draw people to us like a magnet ☐
b) We feel good about ourselves ☐
c) We are motivated ☐
d) All of the above ☐

9. Each of us has which of the following?
a) Phenomenal ability ☐
b) The ability to motivate ourselves ☐
c) The ability to motivate others ☐
d) All of the above ☐

10. Knowledge without action does what?
a) It feels good ☐
b) It's healthy ☐
c) It's meaningful ☐
d) It creates no change ☐

MONDAY

Reverse 'limitation thinking'

Today we'll look at the enormous power we have within us: the power of the mind to help us reach goals. We have the power within us to change any situation, both in life and within an organization.

Three major roadblocks to success and high performance are:

- 'limitation thinking'
- resistance
- problem orientation.

We'll learn to reverse the 'limitation thinking' that sets in so early in life and limits our success. We'll also learn how to overcome resistance to change by turning 'fear thinking' into 'inspiration thinking'.

We'll learn how to envision ideal situations – perhaps completely different from those we are in now – in order to examine roadblocks and see ways to overcome them. You'll also learn how to 'light a fire' under others – employees or family members – who want to achieve something new and important for themselves.

Finally, you'll learn what research shows about negativity in meetings and how to reduce it by giving more time to solutions and less time to the causes of the problems.

The power of the mind

The power of the mind to help us reach our goal is enormous. It's there; we need only to use it. The following true story will give you insight into the power we have available.

A woman from Thailand had been enjoying her holiday in Croatia, and was resting in her car parked on a cliff edge while her companions were hiking.

She was in the back seat when she noticed that the handbrake was not set, and leaned forward to secure it. At that moment, the shift of weight in the small car caused it to roll forward and within a few seconds she was tumbling down the cliff to what she was sure would be death by drowning in the sea far below.

As she rolled over and over, the car banged against the rocks. Her life flashed in front of her and she knew that death was near. There seemed to be no escape.

Suddenly, in the turmoil, she remembered her deep belief that we have the power within us to change any situation. Could it be applied to this, she wondered? Then she focused every fragment of energy she had left to see if she could make any changes to her situation. All the while the car continued to crash down the cliff.

The instant she focused on change, her mind brought forward an idea. If she were able to open the door and put her foot out to keep it open, then she would be able to escape from the car when it hit the water. She tried and, after several difficult attempts, she managed to do it.

Miraculously, she escaped death. After eight long months of hospitalization, she had her life back in order again. She is certain that without her change in focus, deciding that she had the power to change the situation, she would be dead.

Consider her thoughts as you read them again, because they are the decisive words:

'She decided she had the power to change the situation.'

Most of us are not tumbling off cliffs to our death. The crises we face are mundane by comparison, but the power within us to change our situation is the same.

What changes do you want?

Take time to think for a moment of what changes you want to create.

The Thai woman decided on an action that was different from her previous action. That was opening the door, despite heavy resistance from tumbling and turning, and putting her foot out for a brace with the risk of losing it to save her life.

In the mundane events of life, we often do the opposite. We give away our life to save our foot. The things that we really want, we sacrifice. We give away the treasures of life, and the possibility of finding our real potential, for the sake of staying in our comfort zone.

Overturn 'limitation thinking'

What would you do if you knew you couldn't fail at anything? Studies show that 'limitation thinking' about ourselves comes into play between the ages of 6 and 12. If you ask children at age 6 if they think they can succeed at something, 90 per cent say yes. At the age of 12, only 10 per cent say yes. Think about this as you work with people. You may have all the confidence in the world, but perhaps *they* don't.

Here's a process that can put you and them in touch with the visions that existed in life before they were tarnished with 'limitation thinking' and roadblocks.

Just clear your mind for a moment and imagine a fantasy in which your fairy godmother has told you that you can be anything you want. Anything. She's told you not to worry about limitations of money. Don't worry about education or any other limitation. You can be anything you want. Trust her, she says. She will make it all possible.

Imagine, now, waking up in the morning as the ideal you. What qualities do you have?

Imagine the room you wake up in. See the light coming in. See the colours, see the size of the room, see how it's decorated. Listen for the sounds inside and outside.

Now see yourself sitting up in bed and putting your feet on the floor. What do you feel? Carpet, wood, tiles or what?

See yourself getting up and walking to your wardrobe, knowing that 'when you open it' you'll see all the clothes that you really want for your perfect, ideal life. Now open it. What do you see? How do you feel about yourself?

Imagine that this is a weekday and that you are getting ready to do exactly the kind of work you want to do. You choose the clothes for it and get ready to go.

As you leave the house, you look around you. Where are you? Are you in the country or the city? Do you see trees? Do you see streets, rivers, streams, what? Remember, you can be *anything* you want.

Now, see yourself getting to your place of work and 'as you arrive' think of the ideal people you choose to work with. What are their personalities like? What are they doing? *Imagine walking in to your own place of work and see yourself preparing for the day.* Think of your day and what you are doing for ideal job satisfaction.

Now imagine your evening, just as you want it to be. Where do you go? Who are you with? Is it a quiet evening? Are you with friends? Are you relaxing? See your life as you really would like it.

The next day you wake up and discover it's the first day of your ideal holiday. Imagine your excitement. Where are you going? Think of the most idyllic way to spend your time, without limitations.

Your vision might be possible

Come back to this moment and record the key visions that come to you in a table like the one below. What qualities did you have? How did you feel about yourself? What did your home look like? What was your ideal occupation? Where did you go for your holiday?

Key visions	
1	
2	
3	
4	
5	
6	
7	
8	
9	
10	

Now pick two aspects of your vision that you could aim to achieve over a three- or five-year period. Pick one in your professional life and one in your personal life. Record them in a table like the one below. Then think of three probable roadblocks that stand in your way and the actions you can take to overcome them. See what you get. It might be easier than you think.

	Professional aspiration	Personal aspiration
Roadblocks	1 2 3	1 2 3
Actions to overcome roadblocks	1 2 3	1 2 3

Keep these points in mind all day, and you'll have an excellent chance of achieving them.

You can do it

In an audiotape interview with Janet Lim, whom I featured in *Secrets of the World's Top Sales Performers*, I asked what advice she would give to any manager or any parent who wanted to inspire others to reach their highest potential.

She thought for a moment then answered, 'You should tell them, "You can do it, you can do it, you can do it!"' She said we might have to repeat it six or seven times.

It doesn't matter whether they are facing a new job, a new habit they want to acquire or even their maths homework assignment. She is convinced that the first step to success is the belief that we can succeed.

Yet in order to break out of our comfort zone, we usually have to give the 'you can do it' message to ourselves.

Give yourself the message

Take one young man, Tony, who told me he wanted to be a film producer. He had achieved great success in his film class, yet when he told his parents of this success, they remarked derogatorily, 'That's nice, Tony. What were your marks?' To make matters worse, when he told his cousin, the response was 'Who, you? A film producer?'

His parents wanted him to be a plumber. While meaning well, they weren't supporting his vision and talent in life.

TIP

If we want to change our patterns to lead to greater success, we have to give the 'you can do it' message – to ourselves and to others – not once, but often!

Stop the resistance

When we are holding ourselves back, we have to analyse why we are doing it.

Fear versus inspiration

In a motivation seminar I gave in London recently, I told the attendees to notice the difference between fear and inspiration. One holds us back; the other propels us forward.

For example, one woman said she had a fear of speaking out at large meetings. I asked her what she feared. Her answer was, 'They might think I'm foolish.'

I responded, 'On the other hand, a younger woman might see you as a role model, or perhaps there would be an important executive in the room who would respect you and think, "I want to have her on our team." Isn't that a possibility? Wouldn't you also feel better about yourself?'

'Yes,' she said. I could see that my analysis had given her a new perspective and infinitely more courage.

Analysis for change

Fear thinking: They may think I'm foolish.

Inspiration thinking: I might inspire a younger person, or a colleague might respect me for my courage and conviction. Plus I know I'll feel good about myself when I do it.

The more we practise expanding the comfort zone in one area of life, the easier it is to expand it into other areas.

Take a moment now to question again. What would you do in life if you knew you couldn't fail at anything?

Action steps

	What would you really like to do?	What's holding you back?	Action required to break out
A			
B			
C			

The management application

Here's the situation that exists in management. Research has proven that our time spent in meetings breaks down like this: 80 per cent discussing problems and causes of problems, but only 20 per cent on possible solutions. When the researchers looked at it more closely, they discovered even more disconcerting news, as this table shows.

Time spent in meetings

80%	Problems
	Causes of problems
20%	Possible solutions (15–20%)
	Best solutions (0–5%)

When managers become aware of this, they are usually quite appalled and recognize immediately the need for change. Armed with this information, they go back to their colleagues, make them aware of the statistics, and put a new emphasis on meeting agendas. They try to reverse the time spent in meetings so that only 20 per cent is spent discussing problems

SUNDAY
MONDAY
TUESDAY
WEDNESDAY
THURSDAY
FRIDAY
SATURDAY

and their causes and the remaining 80 per cent is devoted to considering solutions.

They realize that, while we cannot ignore a problem, the problem should not consume us. We must learn what we can from the problem and then focus the majority of our time, energy and mental resources on the solution. Soon it becomes a habit to focus on solutions rather than problems alone.

Think of areas of your life or business in which the focus on problems blinds the path to solutions.

The corporation is nothing more than a composite of individuals. They each bring their own strength with them, but also their 'limitation' thinking. It's our job as managers to reverse this.

Think now of problem areas that exist for you. Perhaps they've existed for some time. What action can you take to create a move towards 'solutions thinking'? Consider the following.

Steps to solution leadership

1 Make people aware of the above statistics.
2 Commit to spending more meeting time on solutions.
3 Examine logical roadblocks.
4 Examine psychological roadblocks.
5 Visualize what solution there would be if there were no limitations, then see which solutions can be implemented.
6 Don't let discussion drift away from solutions.
7 Take a few moments now to list three actions you'll take at future meetings.

-
-
-

This reversal towards possibilities and solutions can be applied to decision making in both business and personal life.

TIP *To be highly motivated we need to believe that there is virtually no roadblock that can't be overcome with flexibility, creativity and determination.*

People skills in action

Use an actions table like the one below to enhance your own techniques and achievements. Ideas for development include the following.

1 Decide which areas of limitation thinking are blocking you from reaching your goals.
2 Where would you work, what would you do and where would your life take you if you could be anything you wanted to be?
3 Think about how long it has been since you 'took the plunge' for something you really want.
4 Analyse limitation thinking at meetings. Decide what you can and will do to change it.
5 Complete other points as they relate to you or your organization, according to your needs.

Create your answers

● Of the above ideas, which one is likely to yield the best results for you?
● What percentage performance increase could you realistically expect?
● How long would it take:
    – to develop the idea?
    – to get results?
● Who would have to be involved?
● What date should you start?
● What is the first step you should take?

Actions I will take

Reverse limitation thinking	
Overcome resistance	
Change problem orientation	

Summary

Today we looked at 'limitation thinking' and the power people have within them to change.

Perhaps you want to reverse 'limitation thinking'. Perhaps you have a child, a spouse or an employee you want to motivate. Perhaps you want to eliminate resistance in your organization or make management meetings shorter and multiply their effectiveness. Or perhaps you want to change an organization from problem to solution orientation.

Once you start to employ the methods and skills we've outlined today and carry out the practical activities, you'll find that all of these things are not only possible but also highly likely to be achieved in a very short time.

Tomorrow we'll add to your people skills by looking at how you can raise confidence and self-esteem, in yourself and others.

SUNDAY

MONDAY

TUESDAY

WEDNESDAY

THURSDAY

FRIDAY

SATURDAY

Fact-check (answers at the back)

1. How important is the mind in helping people reach their goal?
   a) It's of limited use ☐
   b) It's hugely powerful ☐
   c) It's useless ☐
   d) None of the above ☐

2. Why do we often sacrifice our true potential?
   a) For good reasons ☐
   b) To please our parents ☐
   c) To stay in our comfort zone ☐
   d) To ease our conscience ☐

3. If you ask children at age 6 if they think they can succeed at something, 90% say yes. At the age of 12, what percentage says yes?
   a) 40% ☐
   b) 20% ☐
   c) 10% ☐
   d) 5% ☐

4. What should you do with your visions to aim for in your personal and professional life?
   a) Record them and then forget about them ☐
   b) Record them and memorize them ☐
   c) Think of probable roadblocks and actions to overcome them ☐
   d) Tell everyone and get support ☐

5. To convince others that they can achieve something, what might you have to tell them repeatedly?
   a) Not to worry ☐
   b) That they can do it ☐
   c) To be brave ☐
   d) To be strong and not give up ☐

6. What often causes people to hold themselves back?
   a) Fear ☐
   b) Inspiration ☐
   c) Panic ☐
   d) Habit ☐

7. Research shows that time in meetings tends to focus on problems and their causes, but only what percentage on possible solutions?
   a) 10% ☐
   b) 20% ☐
   c) 40% ☐
   d) 80% ☐

8. For a better way to get results, what should we focus more time on?
   a) Problems ☐
   b) Causes of problems ☐
   c) Possible solutions and best solution ☐
   d) None of the above ☐

9. What action can you take to move towards 'solutions thinking'?
a) Make people aware of the 80/20 statistic ❏
b) Commit to spending more meeting time on solutions ❏
c) Don't let discussion drift away from solutions ❏
d) All of the above ❏

10. Where can the 'possibilities and solutions approach' to decision making be applied?
a) In both business and personal life ❏
b) In business life only ❏
c) In personal life only ❏
d) None of the above ❏

SUNDAY

MONDAY

TUESDAY

WEDNESDAY

THURSDAY

FRIDAY

SATURDAY

TUESDAY

Elevate
self-esteem
and
confidence

Have you ever wanted instantly to raise someone's performance level, or even your own? In business and in personal life we often need to develop people's potential quickly. We need to discover their transferable skills. We can do this by raising their self-esteem and confidence levels, if we know how.

To address these issues I devised 'the small book method' of confidence building. The process has since proved itself with hundreds of people around the world – perhaps thousands, if you count readers of this book.

Today you'll learn what the process involves and challenge yourself to try it. After two weeks you'll see the results for yourself.

You can use the small book method on yourself as well as with other people. It can be used as a people skills tool in the following areas:

- self-esteem
- employee confidence building
- finding the positive side of life.

The small book method

The process itself is deceptively simple, and yet it has profound impact. Don't let its simplicity put you off. I've seen it help a dynamic woman in her seventies cherish life again, a university graduate gain confidence at his first job, and I've used it with myself and others to build morale.

To carry out this process you will need:

- a small notebook dedicated to this exercise, which fits in the pocket or handbag
- five minutes per day, every day for two weeks, ideally at the end of the working day.

The small book exercise

The small book method came into being after a young intern came to me straight out of university for a summer job. He proved to be a reliable and keen employee, but his performance level was low – understandably so, as it's difficult to transfer college skills to the training and consulting world. He must have felt like a fish out of water.

I needed to raise his confidence levels quickly and make him feel comfortable talking with our client CEOs. Most importantly, I had to make him a productive member of the team. I bought my intern a small lined notebook in which to record his findings for the exercise – hence the name.

You're likely to start seeing results as early as the third day, and the effect of two complete weeks has a positive visible impact for several years.

Try it now on yourself and see what you get. Then you'll be in a position to 'sell' the idea to other people. Start the process as follows.

1 Sit down at the end of a working day and reflect on the day's events.
2 Find two events you enjoyed or got a sense of satisfaction from and record these.

The small book method for raising self-esteem

After you record your two points for the day, ask yourself this question.

'What quality do I have which enabled me to enjoy that or to get a sense of satisfaction from it?'

Jot the quality down at the bottom of the page. Choose any word that seems right to you. It could be persistence, caring about people, creativity, love of challenge, sensitivity, communication skill, curiosity and so on. Now close the book. You're finished for today.

Tomorrow, at the same time of day, review that day's events and choose another two that you enjoyed or from which you got satisfaction. Record these and decide what quality you had which enabled you to enjoy it. The quality can be the same or different from the day before.

Look for trends
By the third day you'll have six events and qualities and you'll start to see a trend building.

'Put your future in good hands - your own.'

Anon.

Self-esteem progress

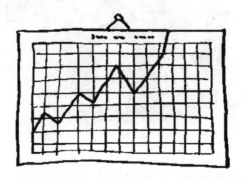

Look for the common factors in what you enjoyed and got satisfaction from. Did you like talking with people? If so, what was it that you enjoyed? Was it negotiating? Was it helping them find solutions? Was it the camaraderie of being in a team?

By the end of the two weeks you'll have a clear understanding of your strengths and what you enjoy. You will have a new and positive insight about yourself. This knowledge will have a profound impact on your self-esteem.

Case study

Karen was in her thirties and wanted to interview for a meaningful job leading to a career in management, after some years out of the workforce raising children. Her self-esteem was far lower than she would have liked it to be.

She was afraid to pick up the telephone to prospective employers and job placement agencies. She used the small book process because she felt she needed to raise her self-esteem in order to convince herself of her marketable value before she could convince someone else.

Here are her recordings. What trend do you see?

	Day 1	Day 2	Day 3
Enjoyment/ satisfaction events	1 Read psychology book and got new idea to implement 2 Enjoyed phone call with cabinet maker regarding modifications	1 Enjoyed talking with new person at adult education class 2 Satisfaction from reorganizing driving schedule of three parents, with co-operation from all	1 Great satisfaction from speaking up at committee meeting to bring subject back on track 2 Enjoyed organizing German-speaking get-together
Qualities relating to above	1 Good at focusing on implementation 2 Good at creating solutions	1 Realization that I initiated the meeting and conversation 2 Working with people to create solutions	1 Ability to see main purpose. Ability to lead others 2 Ability to organize people and initiate events

After only three days she had undeniable evidence that she was good at implementing ideas, organizing events, clarifying purpose and leading people. These are perfect management skills.

After 14 days the evidence was even more undeniable, and she actually had more than sufficient self-esteem to approach prospective employers and agencies. She reported having more self-esteem than she could ever remember having.

The small book method for confidence building

Let's look at ways to use the process with employees. Your situation could be similar to the one that I faced when I hired the university graduate I mentioned earlier. This was his first professional job. After one week I noticed that his confidence was not as high as it needed to be to talk to senior executives on the telephone.

I didn't have time for him to 'grow into the job': I needed him to take a giant leap. I wanted him to transfer his skills from university life to the job at once. Here's how I did it, taking five minutes a day with the small book method for a confidence-building process.

Let them pinpoint their own strengths

First I explained the process, saying that the purpose was for him to discover his own strengths. Then I explained exactly how to review the day and choose two things he enjoyed or got self-satisfaction from. I stressed that the two points should definitely be what he himself valued, not what he thought I would value.

A few minutes later I reviewed the list with him. That was important because I was looking for events and qualities that could prove to John that he was good at speaking with high-level executives on the telephone, which is what was needed from him.

Here's how it progressed. John came to me with the following.

	Day 1
Enjoyment/satisfaction events	1 Enjoyed finding suitable prospective customers from Chamber of Commerce trade mission lists 2 Felt good about sitting in on meeting with Mr Barrett

On the first day I helped him identify the related qualities: 'This is interesting – identifying the prospective customers. What did you like about it?'

John answered, 'I liked trying to figure out which ones were most likely to need our service. I looked at their industry and the details about their company.'

'What does that tell you about yourself?' I asked.

'Hm, I suppose I like fact finding.'

'Yes, I agree. And that's an important quality in dealing with high-level executives. They will value that in you when you work with them.'

John wrote down 'Good at fact finding' as the first quality.

Let them record it

By letting the employee write it down, you will be helping him or her reinforce their qualities and thus their confidence. It is he or she, not you, who needs the quick confidence building.

'Now let's look at point two,' I said. 'What was it that you liked about sitting in on the meeting with Mr Barrett?'

'I suppose I liked trying to figure out why he was here and what he hoped to gain,' answered John.

'Ah,' I interjected. 'That's very important. I'm glad you've seen that about yourself. Imagine how happy these executives will feel about talking with you because you're trying to figure out what they need. This is a great help to them. What more could they ask?'

Some time later John told me that he left the office that night on such a high that he couldn't sleep.

His enthusiasm the next day was boundless. He reasoned that I was his boss, so if I believed in him, he should believe in himself. After all, I should know. After three or four days of this there was no holding him back. I practically needed two telephones to keep him going. (That young man went on to become a company executive and eventually start his own successful business.)

Choose the correct strength

Naturally, with an employee you'll choose a confidence-building area that your department needs. But you need not feel too selfish about this because the confidence area you choose to work on will spread to other areas of your employee's job and life. You'll get higher performance; the employee will increase his or her self-development and satisfaction with life.

When you use this process:

● you gain
● the employee gains
● the organization gains.

Discovering the positive side of life

A dynamic client of mine attended my seminar on confidence building and decided to apply it to seeing life in a more positive way.

I knew her to be a very positive person, and I wondered frankly whether the process could help her, as I didn't see much room for improvement.

After a few days she called me to say that she was astounded with her findings. On the first day she sat for 20 minutes reviewing the day. She could find nothing positive, nothing she enjoyed, nothing satisfying. The day, as she saw it, had been full of problems to be solved and annoyances to be overcome. For 20 minutes she probed and probed and found nothing – absolutely nothing. She was ready to give up.

Suddenly another thing popped into her mind – a letter she had received from a treasured friend abroad, reminiscing about their recent time together. She remembered that, as she had read the letter, she had been filled with gratitude for the excitement of life and friendship. Next, she remembered another positive event, and then another.

She wondered how the negative points of her day could have blocked the memory of the day's positive points in her mind for 20 minutes. It seemed impossible. This realization heightened her determination to keep at the process.

The next night she reported that the negative factors again predominated, but not for as long a period. Again, she was astounded at how the mind could be so stubbornly stuck to the negative when, in fact, there was so much that was good. Yet, by pushing these back, the mind leaves us in a negative mental spiral.

Firm up the muscles of the mind

She persisted with the process for a third day and found that she could now more easily bring the positive events up in her mind. She decided that the process of positive recall in the brain is analogous to muscles in the body that need firming up. Without use, they become weak and ineffective.

I've had feedback from many other seminar attendees and readers from age 17 to 70, attesting to the effectiveness of the process. I still use it myself from time to time if the doldrums start to settle in, or if I want to raise my excitement for day-to-day life.

The conclusion is this. If a person who was already very positive benefited from this process, imagine the benefits that await the rest of us.

Where to apply it

Take today to decide with whom you will use this motivation process. Will it be with yourself or with others? Think also of the outcome desired: self-esteem, confidence building, finding the positive side of life.

Application

Who (self/others)	Outcome desired

 TIP

Remember that you have the power within you to influence your world around you.

People skills in action

Use an actions table like the one below to enhance your own techniques and achievements. Ideas for development include the following.

1 Build your own self-esteem with this method.
2 Raise employees' confidence.
3 Heighten your morale.
4 Look for trends in your strengths.
5 Encourage employees to pinpoint their own strengths with this method.
6 Complete other points as they relate to you, according to your needs.

Create your answers

● Of the above ideas, which one is likely to yield the best results for you?
● What percentage performance increase could you realistically expect?

- How long would it take:
  - to develop the idea
  - to get results?
- Who would have to be involved?
- What date should you start?
- What is the first step you should take?

Actions I will take

Raise self-esteem	
Build employee confidence	
Find the positive side of life	

Summary

Today you learned an easy and amazingly fast method for building confidence and self-esteem in yourself and others. It's also useful for raising the performance level of young or less confident employees so that they can achieve greater results.

The process for employees involves recording two events each day for two weeks that the person enjoyed or got a sense of satisfaction from. After only a few days of recording two events, both you and the employee will see a pattern developing. You'll see areas of interest and strengths that might otherwise take months to discover, and that sometimes go unnoticed for a lifetime.

This will allow you as the employer to capitalize on those skills and to have a happy, productive and loyal employee. The same process is used when you do it for yourself.

This process is also extremely effective in helping people discover the positive side of life, thus raising their morale and enthusiasm for life. I also highly recommend it for discovering your potential. Often we have undiscovered skills, talents and interests. With this process you are certain to recognize them and – who knows – it may start you on a new path in life!

SUNDAY MONDAY TUESDAY WEDNESDAY THURSDAY FRIDAY SATURDAY

Fact-check (answers at the back)

1. What can the confidence-building process be used for?
   a) Raising self-esteem ❑
   b) Building employee confidence ❑
   c) Finding the positive side of life ❑
   d) All of the above ❑

2. How much time does the confidence-building process take?
   a) Five minutes a day for two weeks ❑
   b) Five minutes a day for two months ❑
   c) Ten minutes a day for a week ❑
   d) Fifteen minutes a day ❑

3. With this process, how soon are you likely to start seeing results?
   a) By the first day ❑
   b) By the third day ❑
   c) By the seventh day ❑
   d) By the tenth day ❑

4. To use the process, what two things will you need to find each day?
   a) Things you did well ❑
   b) Things completed on time ❑
   c) Things you enjoyed or got a sense of satisfaction from ❑
   d) Things you excelled at and brought to the attention of your boss ❑

5. After you record your two points for the day, what question do you need to ask yourself?
   a) Why did I enjoy that and get a sense of satisfaction from it? ❑
   b) What would my boss most appreciate about that? ❑
   c) Who can I talk to about this to get motivated? ❑
   d) What quality do I have which enables me to enjoy or get a sense of satisfaction from it? ❑

6. By the third day of using this process, how many events and qualities that indicate your strengths will you have?
   a) Three ❑
   b) Six ❑
   c) Nine ❑
   d) Twelve ❑

7. In using this process with employees, when should you sit down with them for five minutes each day?
   a) In the morning ❑
   b) At lunch ❑
   c) At the end of the working day ❑
   d) None of the above ❑

8. What is the purpose of using the process with employees?
   a) For them to discover their own strengths ❑
   b) For the personnel department to discover their strengths ❑
   c) For their family to discover their strengths ❑
   d) None of the above ❑

9. What's the best way to get fast results with the process?
a) Let the employee write down their own qualities daily ☐
b) Write it down for them daily ☐
c) Let them do it at home weekly ☐
d) Let them do it as they choose ☐

10. When using the process to find the positive side of life, what do you need to keep in mind?
a) Some days have no positive events ☐
b) You need a good memory to do the process ☐
c) On the first day or two it might be difficult to remember the positive events of the day ☐
d) None of the above ☐

SUNDAY

MONDAY

TUESDAY

WEDNESDAY

THURSDAY

FRIDAY

SATURDAY

WEDNESDAY

Reinforce strengths – eliminate weaknesses

How many teachers or managers have you had who really motivated you, who encouraged you or showed you the positive within yourself? You may have had one or two. Few people know how to make others see the best in themselves. Those who do have people who will follow them anywhere because this is such a rare and treasured commodity – all based on the skill of positive reinforcement.

Today you'll learn how to master this skill in three easy steps. In working with thousands of seminar attendees around the world, we've developed a three-part process for reinforcing strengths and eliminating weaknesses, which is effective with every culture, every age group and every industry group. You can use it in many different contexts to reap high rewards.

The three-part process is as follows.

1 Tell the other person what they did correctly.
2 Tell them how the action helped you.
3 Express your appreciation.

You'll see today how you can use the process in business and everyday life to deflect negativity and enhance your effectiveness with employees, volunteers, the boss and friends and family members too.

The positive reinforcement process

On the following pages you'll find examples of applying the process in six different situations. Use these for inspiration for your own people. Undoubtedly, you'll think of people and situations as you read these. Jot down the names and ideas so that you can implement them immediately.

The chances are that the rewards to yourself of practising positive reinforcement will be greater than you can imagine. Once you start it, you will want to use it in every situation.

The four steps in practising the process are as follows.

1 Choose several people from your business or personal life who you want to motivate.
2 Write out a statement of positive reinforcement for each from the following pages.
3 Test the process on an ad lib basis with those around you who are not on the list in order to build your expertise – the children, the caretaker, the dog, the postman.
4 Telephone two from your list and give the reinforcement. The reaction you'll get will be so reinforcing for you that you'll continue without hesitation.

The three-part process

1 Tell the other person exactly what action they did correctly.
2 Tell them how the action helped you or the organization.
3 Express your honest and sincere appreciation.

You can reverse the order of points two and three, depending on how it suits you and the situation. You can thank them and then tell them how it helped or vice versa.

As well as increasing motivation, this process also leads to loyalty – and in a big way. I've taught this process around the world with extraordinary results – from sessions with the US military, to corporate audiences in Europe, America and Asia.

After one keynote speech I gave about the process for IBM in Monte Carlo, a business owner told me how he applied the method and the results he got. Apparently, the method made him think of his most valued employee, and during lunch he called his office to express his appreciation, only to discover that this employee felt undervalued and was thinking of leaving the company. However, because of the call and the boss's use of the three-part reinforcement process, the employee decided to stay on – much to the relief of my audience member.

The performance focus

The situation is this. We have an employee who is important in the chain of events, but one of his skill areas falls short of the required performance. This is his lack of attention to detail.

Each time he communicates a message, there is an error in it caused by this lack of attention to detail. We find that packages are going to wrong addresses at the wrong time, messages are getting confused and so on.

He is valuable in other skill areas such as making good contact with people and we want to help him improve in this area of detail in order to meet the job requirements. Our objective is to motivate him, not *demotivate* him.

We look for even the *slightest* improvement or any sign that he's handled detail better. Then we use the three-part process.

The process: raising performance

● **Repeat the correct action exactly**

'John, yesterday, when you wrote that list of addresses down, you carefully double-checked them with me,' we say.

● **Express your honest, sincere appreciation**

'I appreciate that extra trouble you took.'

● **Tell them how that action helped you or the organization**

'It will help us to be accurate the first time, and considering how busy we are here, that's vital. Thanks, John.'

The result

The positive reinforcement will only take us 30 seconds to say, but it will linger for hours with the employee.

By acknowledging the correct behaviour, we are drawing attention to it. After we do this two, three or four times, the acknowledgement will be ingrained. The employee will soon be checking the details as a matter of course.

What to avoid

Some people misunderstand the process and think that it's one in which they tell the employee what *should* have been done. Instead of talking about the correct action taken, they discuss the correct action they would like to see.

This is not positive reinforcement. It's another type of communication exercise, which draws attention to what was *not* accomplished. It is reinforcing of negative behaviour, which is demotivating for the employee.

The danger is that they can feel:

● that you are ungrateful for all they have done
● hopelessly unable to achieve.

Both of these feelings are demotivating.

'John, I noticed yesterday that you didn't double-check the addresses with me. You must do this in the future because it's important to be accurate.'

This is not positive reinforcement.

The best way to change behaviour and motivate is to show the employee proof that they have already succeeded and that you endorse what they can do. You prove it by picking an incident in which they have done it. That endorsement leads to more of the same.

The loyalty focus

The situation is this. We have a high-flying sales executive who outperforms the others on the team by 50 per cent and more. She is highly motivated and we know she could move to other jobs for more money or career opportunities. We would like to maintain her performance and keep her with the company.

First, before we give positive reinforcement, we think about her situation and ask ourselves what kind of acknowledgement she wants. She's working hard, has perfected her sales skills and keeps her motivation up.

What is it that really puts her head and shoulders above the rest? We want to give her acknowledgement for this special skill or attribute. We decide that her decisive quality is determination.

Secondly, we know it's important to reinforce only one thing at a time. Since we want to maintain her performance and keep her loyal to the company, we decide to reinforce the determination behind her performance. We then use the three-part process.

The process: raising loyalty

● Repeat the correct action exactly

'Julie, I want to commend you on your consistent high sale results. I know it's not a magical process. It's no accident that you're 50 per cent above everyone else. It takes unrelenting determination to achieve what you've achieved. Determination to make the appointments every day, determination to close every sale, determination to keep perfecting skills,' we say.

● Tell them how that action helped you or the organization

'That's a wonderful role model for the others on the team. They may never be able to reach your level but, step by step, by seeing your determination, they'll be able to improve their own determination and improve their results and job satisfaction.'

● Express your honest, sincere appreciation

'Thanks for your contribution, Julie. We're lucky to have you on our team.'

The result

It's said that, if we show people the best in themselves, they will follow us anywhere. We know that a definite outcome of our intervention will be that she'll feel loyalty to us for seeing the best in her.

> ### Remember
> The world around us is full of people who are used to expressing negativity and doubt. Many are contained in their own shell, their energy going towards self-survival. You might be the only person who develops the skill to motivate the people around you.

The anti-negativity focus

The situation is this. We go to a committee meeting for a fund-raising project, and there is much diversity of opinion about the venue, the ticket price, and even the date of the event. The chairman is ready to throw his hands up in despair and resign the post if people don't consolidate.

One person in particular, Arthur, is a rabble-rouser. While he stated several good ideas, he also stirred up things by wanting to look at the negative side of every suggestion made. As a result, the meeting is having more negative than positive conclusions.

We assess the situation and decide that positive reinforcement is necessary to change the output of the rabble-rouser, otherwise we and the chairman and half of the committee will abandon the project. The committee needs the project, and we want it to succeed. At coffee break, we go to Arthur the rabble-rouser and start a friendly conversation.

In the meantime our mind is racing through the dialogue of the evening, looking for good points to reinforce which meet the group's objective of a positive conclusion. At last we remember one specific action and we use that in the three-part process.

The process: reducing negativity

● **Repeat the correct action exactly**

'Arthur, I was thinking of the time tonight that you supported the chairman, after the majority vote on the venue,' we say.

● **Tell them how that action helped you or the organization**

'I noticed that your support had a positive effect on the group. Everyone felt good to have one thing settled.'

● **Express honest, sincere appreciation**

'Thanks, it's good to work on committees with supportive people because we achieve a lot.'

The result

You may feel that this approach is a bit transparent and that Arthur – or types like him – will see right through it. But remember that many people's behaviour is more subconscious than conscious. So far, the attention they've had in life has been for their inappropriate behaviour, in this case rabble-rousing. We are drawing attention to another behaviour that they can perceive as noble and worthy of consciously repeating.

The participation focus

Voluntary organizations

There are thousands of worthy organizations around us in which people volunteer their time: chambers of commerce, church groups, community groups, charities, committees, service clubs. Think what added impact they could make if their members could be more motivated. Could you be the person to do that?

The situation is this. You have many members who come into your volunteer group and show enthusiasm for the first few months, then fade away. It seems that all the work is left to the same people, year in and year out.

Your goal is to get more people co-operating and giving their time. You just decide that it's time for a change and you take on the challenge yourself.

Starting at baseline '0'

From this point on, you decide that you'll give every member positive reinforcement for some action they've taken. It doesn't matter how small this action was. You start with a baseline of '0', indicating 'zero contribution'. You should consider anything above '0' to be a contribution.

What did each member do? Even attendance by itself is good, because no one *has* to come. They could, in fact, drop out. That's their option if they're not motivated. We're the ones asking for change, not them. We have to do the motivating and loyalty building, and it's important not to be judgmental.

The process: increasing participation

● **Repeat the correct action exactly**
'Ted, thanks for coming tonight,' we say.

● **Express honest, sincere appreciation**
'I know it's tough after a long day at work.'

● **Tell them how that action helped you or the organization**
'It really helps us to succeed when we have busy members like you who make the extra effort to come. Thanks.'

You don't have to be in a position of leadership to motivate people. It can be your unique contribution to the organization. The loyalty and good you will build will be profoundly rewarding. And you become the leader.

Starting above the baseline

In volunteer groups as well as in business, negativity can creep in. People may be contributing regularly and well but feel their work isn't appreciated. It takes positive reinforcement to counter this. You can use the three-part process to make individual members – perhaps those doing committee work – feel more valued through positive acknowledgement of their efforts.

The process: maintaining participation

● **Repeat the correct action exactly**
'Alice, we'd like to thank you for your efforts on the telephone committee,' we say.

● **Tell them how it helped you or the organization**
'At the board meeting last week we discussed the fact that attendance at meetings is up 30 per cent over last year. We're sure it's due to your work on the telephone committee.'

● **Express honest, sincere appreciation**
'Thanks, Alice. I know it's not easy to make the time and we're all very grateful to you.'

The result

It's important to recognize every member's input. I can guarantee that, if you reinforce this, within two months you'll have a completely different atmosphere and enthusiasm level. I've seen it time and time again.

Think now of the groups you belong to. What could you do to be a catalyst for positive change?

The gaining support focus

The situation is this. Your boss is always hassled and you want more time to talk to him or her uninterrupted. Your purpose is to gain support from your boss, so you use the three-part process to reinforce something you like and want more of in the way of support.

The process: gaining support

● Repeat the correct action exactly

'Harry, do you remember three months ago when you took time to go to lunch with me to discuss the Egyptian project?' we say.

● Tell them how it helped you or the organization

'I want you to know how much I valued that chance to talk without interruption. It helped me afterwards to work with more clarity and it speeded up the whole process.'

● Express honest, sincere appreciation

'I know your time is torn in all directions so I wanted to take the opportunity to let you know I appreciated it. Thanks.'

The result

Your boss will certainly appreciate your positive feedback because it's highly likely that he or she doesn't get as much positive recognition as they would like either.

Naturally, this process can be used for anyone you want support from, not only your boss. Just think of a time when they did something that you appreciated in the way of support and reinforce it.

The relationship focus

The situation is this. You're sitting with your partner at a café in Paris or London or Prague or Los Angeles. It crosses your mind that these occasions are too few and far between. You have two choices. You can lambast yourself and your partner

SUNDAY MONDAY TUESDAY WEDNESDAY THURSDAY FRIDAY SATURDAY

for not taking more time alone together or you can use positive reinforcement. Which one is likely to get better results? (Hint: the first way doesn't usually work very well for most people, does it?)

The process: enhancing a relationship

● **Repeat the correct action exactly**
'Isn't it fantastic sitting here like this together? I'm so glad we took the time to do it,' we say.

● **Express your honest, sincere appreciation**
'Thanks for rearranging your schedule so that we could come. I know it took an effort.'

● **How it helped you or the organization**
'It's really great to stop and celebrate now and again. It makes me realize that's what we work for.'

Perfect the process

Here are some tips for perfecting the process as you apply it, whatever the context.

1 Repeat the correct action precisely so that it's clear what action you refer to.
2 Include only the part of the action that you wish to reinforce.
3 Reinforce only one action at a time.

4 Repeat the reinforcement process often. Choose different actions relating to the same performance you wish to reinforce, until you are happy with the level.

5 When the desired level is reached, reinforce occasionally.

Think now of what you want to reinforce, and with whom.

Action steps

Who	
Repeat the correct action exactly	
Tell them how it helped you or the organization	
Express honest, sincere appreciation	

People skills in action

Use an actions table like the one below to enhance your own techniques and achievements. Ideas for development include the following.

1 Use this method to improve employee performance.
2 Use it to build loyalty from others.
3 Use this to turn around negativity.
4 Use it with volunteer and community groups to encourage participation.
5 Use this with your partner to encourage the behaviour you desire.
6 Complete other points as they relate to you, according to your needs.

Create your answers

● Of the above ideas, which one is likely to yield the best results for you?
● What percentage performance increase could you realistically expect?

- How long would it take:
  - to develop the idea
  - to get results?
- Who would have to be involved?
- What date should you start?
- What is the first step you should take?

Actions I will take

Improve employee performance	
Build loyalty	
Reduce negativity	
Encourage participation	
Improve personal relationships	

Summary

Today you learned an incredibly powerful people skills tool, the three-part reinforcement process. You can use it to raise performance, foster loyalty and turn around negativity. You can use it in all situations with all types of people, from employees and volunteers to bosses, family members and partners.

Each part of the process is essential, so resist the temptation to modify or delete any steps. You can change the order of the steps, but you must include them all for the process to be successful. You should:

1 repeat the correct action exactly
2 express honest appreciation
3 tell them how that action helped you or the organization.

Don't let the simplicity of the formula fool you. Some people misread the formula and think they should tell employees what they *should* do, rather than what they have done right. This is not positive reinforcement, and does not yield the desired results.

Think now of a person whose performance you want to raise, whose loyalty you want to foster or whose negativity you want to turn around. Use the formula and stand back in amazement as you watch the results unfold.

Fact-check (answers at the back)

1. What would you use the three-part reinforcement process for?
   a) To improve performance ❑
   b) To build loyalty or turn around negativity ❑
   c) With volunteers, bosses, employees, children or spouses ❑
   d) All of the above ❑

2. How long does the positive reinforcement process take?
   a) Thirty seconds ❑
   b) Three minutes ❑
   c) Ninety seconds ❑
   d) An hour ❑

3. By acknowledging the correct or desired behaviour, what will it become?
   a) A matter of habit ❑
   b) Well practised ❑
   c) Ingrained in the person's mind ❑
   d) A matter of course ❑

4. What do you need to do to use the three-part reinforcement process?
   a) Tell the other person what action they did correctly ❑
   b) Tell them how the action helped you or the organization ❑
   c) Express your honest and sincere appreciation ❑
   d) All of the above ❑

5. What is telling an employee what they *should* have done?
   a) Not positive reinforcement ❑
   b) Positive reinforcement ❑
   c) An essential daily task ❑
   d) None of the above ❑

6. What type of people is the world full of?
   a) Those who love to motivate others ❑
   b) Experts at motivating others ❑
   c) Those who often express positive thoughts ❑
   d) People used to expressing negativity and doubt ❑

7. What is the best way to turn around negative behaviour?
   a) Point out a time they were positive and how it helped the organization ❑
   b) Make a negative comment ❑
   c) Ignore it ❑
   d) Ask someone to speak to them privately ❑

8. How do you improve performance within a volunteer organization?
   a) Be in a leadership position ❑
   b) Use the three-part reinforcement process ❑
   c) Understand everyone's motive ❑
   d) All of the above ❑

9. When thinking of bosses, what should you remember?
   a) They don't get as much positive recognition as they would like ❑
   b) They get plenty of recognition from their bosses ❑
   c) They get plenty of recognition from their employees ❑
   d) All of the above ❑

10. What's the best way to perfect the three-part reinforcement process?

a) Repeat the correct action precisely so that it's clear what action you refer to ❑

b) Include only the part of the action that you wish to reinforce ❑

c) Reinforce only one action at a time ❑

d) All of the above ❑

THURSDAY

Catapult performance

Do you want to motivate your employees, your family or even your local sports team to raise their performance level? If so, you can use a fascinating process used by dolphin trainers for catapulting performance that has proved highly successful with humans as well.

It's not complex: for dolphin trainers it's simply a matter of asking questions such as, 'How high can the dolphin jump now?' and, 'How high do we want it to jump?' Reinforcement is then given at exactly the right moment, and this encourages the dolphin to jump at the higher level more often.

While it's an easy way of raising the performance level of humans too, we must first pay attention to the *current* performance level of the person we want improvement from. We don't expect the dolphin to double the height of its jump in one fell swoop. We first get it to achieve a certain height, stabilize it, and then go for a slightly higher jump and stabilize that, and continue gradually until the goal is reached.

Today we'll look at the process in depth and see how to develop people skills in specific areas to increase performance.

The dolphin process

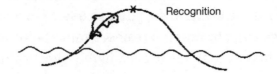

Recognition

In training a dolphin, the trainer analyses its current skill or performance level. The trainer then picks the highest level that the dolphin can jump and waits until the dolphin reaches that level in its jump. When that high point is reached, a whistle is blown. The whistle acts as reinforcement, encouraging the dolphin to achieve that level more often.

- When the dolphin stabilizes at that level, the trainer raises the level at which the whistle is blown.
- When the dolphin reaches that new high level in any jump, the whistle recognition acts as a reinforcement to achieve that higher level more often.
- The trainer repeats the process, stabilizing each level, moving the performance gradually up.

Enhance student performance

Let's look at a variety of ways this can be used to motivate people to raise their performance.

For better progress and enjoyment

One language teacher uses this instant reinforcement to improve the pronunciation of his students in learning foreign languages.

He has a pleasant-sounding buzzer that he rings each time the student pronounces the 'e' sound properly. When the 'e' is stabilized, he moves on to the 'a' sound, and so on. Their progress is fast and they become more encouraged more quickly.

The dropout level of his students is considerably lower than it was before he started the system, his graduates have a reputation for excellence that reflects favourably on his school and, most importantly, his students really enjoy learning. They report much more confidence and motivation.

For faster skill building

When I train instructors to run our courses, I use the system in this way. The instructors each make their presentation and I observe their skills.

First I give them positive feedback on everything they do well in their presentation – voice level, eye contact, friendliness and so on.

Then I choose one area for improvement and they concentrate on that in their next round of presentations. Each time they succeed in the improvement, they get a thumbs-up, signalling success from one of us at the back of the room. When the thumbs-up comes from their fellow trainers as well, the impact increases.

When they reach the level of performance necessary in that area, we change the focus to another area, such as voice modulation or whatever needs improving. Within an extraordinarily short period their skill level moves up.

The process is almost unbelievable. The head of one of our training centres told the new instructors, 'You changed in front of my very eyes. I can hardly believe it's possible.'

Enhance employee performance

One manager used this process to help her employee, Martin, communicate his ideas more often at meetings. The employee was reluctant to speak out for fear of being wrong or being ridiculed, yet his ideas were often superior to those of his colleagues.

Without telling him what the desired performance was, the manager drafted an improvement schedule for what she hoped she could motivate him to achieve.

The schedule looked like this, stage by stage.

1 Speak out, even one to five words: stabilize.
2 Express an opinion: stabilize.
3 Express a complete idea or suggestion: stabilize.
4 Defend his position: stabilize.
5 Make a presentation: stabilize.
6 Make a presentation and take questions afterwards, defending his position: stabilize.

At the next meeting she watched carefully for any comment he might make. Her goal, remember, was to reinforce even one to five words he might say. She knew from past experience that this was likely to be his maximum performance level. Finally it came. After one colleague expressed his view, Martin added, 'Yes, I've observed that too.'

Give instant reinforcement

She was quick to give instant reinforcement. She said to the group, 'Martin has observed that too. That's important. Now let's delve into this issue further. If anyone has any observations on this area during the week, I would like a report back on it. Thank you, Martin.'

Thus his speaking out was reinforced. After several meetings he was speaking out more readily and so she decided it was time to move her reinforcement of his achievements up to stage two, that of expressing his opinion. She waited for that and when it came she reinforced it in a similar way as she had for stage one.

She continued stage by stage to stabilize each performance, then moved the reinforcement up to a higher plateau.

Her planning and reinforcement stages for Martin are illustrated in this diagram.

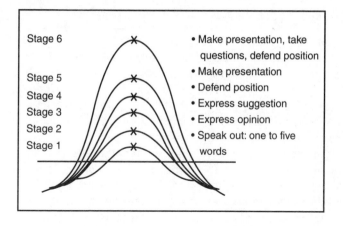

Stage 6   • Make presentation, take questions, defend position

Stage 5   • Make presentation

Stage 4   • Defend position

Stage 3   • Express suggestion

Stage 2   • Express opinion

Stage 1   • Speak out: one to five words

Stabilize each stage

Two important aspects of the process, as shown in the above example, are that you must:

● plan your reinforcement levels ahead of time
● stick with the reinforcement of each stage until you are confident it is stabilized.

The manager understood the importance of reinforcing the first stage securely. This required the most patience on her part. After that, progress was quicker. For this employee:

● the first stage required six reinforcements
● the second stage required four
● the third required three
● the fourth required three
● the fifth required two
● the sixth required two.

After that, the manager gave him sporadic reinforcement, which maintained the level.

Thus we see that, with a total of only 20 reinforcements, the employee went from inadequate to excellent in his verbal contributions. That's an incredible feat, hardly achievable with any other known method.

The importance of planning

Think about the process and see what you observe to be the key elements. Where would it be likely to fall apart? What pressure points should we watch for?

The planning of the stages is certainly important. Notice, for example, that the manager chose to reinforce Martin's expression of a suggestion and his expression of an opinion as two different stages. This builds confidence.

Had she tried to achieve the same results with only four stages of reinforcement with that employee, without such finely divided increments, he might not have succeeded. However, with another employee possessing more skill or confidence, she may have been able to use only four increment stages, either leaving out some or starting her reinforcement at stage three.

Set the level right

Thus it's important to put emphasis on our planning of increments, making each level achievable for each particular employee, according to their skill and confidence level.

Think about the people you might want to motivate to a higher performance level. Are there members of your firm, family, community or clubs? Whose skill or performance level do you want to enhance?

Take today to write the ideal skill or performance level you would like them to achieve, and then list the increments you could reinforce, using a plan like this one.

Application plan

	Person 1	Person 2
Name		
Ideal skill level to achieve		
Increments to reinforce		

How long to reinforce

Many people worry that the reinforcement will have to go on for ever. They also worry that the skill area or behaviour will slip backwards without reinforcement.

Fortunately, this is not the case. Once we learn to ride a bicycle, we don't need to ride it every day. Now and again is enough. So it is with reinforcement.

Improve your own performance

The following is an example of how someone applied the process to improve their own situation. As you read it, you might be tempted to think it's a trivial issue, not worth bothering about. But remember that life is really a composite of individual issues. If we can improve one issue dramatically, as Jenny did, it impacts positively on us and on the people around us.

Note the care Jenny took to analyse her situation and plan each increment accordingly. It's important to do this no matter what your performance issue might be.

Jenny's problem was that she woke up in a negative frame of mind every morning. It took her a good 45 minutes before she was ready to face the world.

She hated this way of starting the day and decided to use the dolphin process to see if she could change her situation. Her target was to have 30 seconds or less of negativity each morning instead of 45 minutes.

She analysed the thoughts and actions of her negative frame of mind in order to figure out how to reverse each one.

These were her irrational thoughts, which seemed rational when her alarm went off:

- Oh, no!
- I can't handle the day. Too much to do, not enough time.
- Why am I in this situation? I want to escape.
- It's too much effort to get dressed.
- I never have time for anything I really want to do.

She then set up the following stage increments.

Block out negativity: stage 1

Jenny decided that she needed to start with blocking out all negative thoughts until she had had her first sip of coffee. She bought a timer for her coffee machine so that a cup of coffee would be ready for her as soon as she woke up.

Block out negativity: stage 2

Then she moved up to her next increment: 'Don't worry about getting dressed until after your shower.'

Block out negativity: stage 3

Then she decided on her third increment: 'Get oxygen flowing to brain.' She would go straight from the shower to a window, open it and take a few deep breaths.

Block out negativity: stage 4

Still she wasn't sure these three steps were enough. She also knew that, once she was involved in a task that engaged her mind, she was fine.

She remembered that she liked to write short thank-you notes to friends but felt she never had time. She decided to make that her fourth stage. This would engage her mind without taxing it with decisions. She reckoned that the time she usually spent feeling depressed could be diverted to this task and she could still leave the house with plenty of time to get to work.

Make a schedule

Next, Jenny planned how many days it would take to stabilize each stage. Her projection looked like this.

Stage 1 (6 days)	Coffee – think of nothing else
Stage 2 (6 days)	Coffee and shower – think of nothing else
Stage 3 (10 days)	Coffee, shower and fresh air – think of nothing else
Stage 4 (4 days)	Coffee, shower, fresh air, write thank-you note

It seemed like a lot of work, but she didn't like the alternative of waking up each morning in such a negative frame of mind. She was motivated by the realization that, if she stuck with the old system, over the same period of 26 days, she would have accumulated 19½ hours of demotivating misery. It was therefore worth a try.

Jenny's results were even better than her prediction. By the second day she was doing the coffee, the shower and the thank-you note. She said that it seemed that, by having a positive, step-by-step progression of things to do, the mind was keen to move from one to the next.

Try this exercise

Take a minute now to think of how you could apply the process to your own situation. What performance or achievement level would you like to reach?

Action plan

Ideal level to achieve	
Increments	
Predicted repetitions needed	

In this self-application process, you have to be both coach and subject. Because you have to be your own coach, you'll have to set everything up ahead of time. Make a list and get everything ready for every stage before you start stage 1.

In Jenny's case she had to prepare for stage 1 by buying a timer for the coffee maker and then filling it the night before. She also had to put the thank-you notes in a readily accessible place.

Take today to think about this process and decide how else to use it. Will it be with colleagues, with yourself, or both? Decide when and what to do.

People skills in action

Use an actions table like the one below to enhance your own techniques and achievements. Ideas for development include the following.

1 Use this method for faster skill building, better progress and enjoyment.
2 Remember to give instant reinforcement.
3 Stabilize each stage.
4 Set the right level for reinforcement.
5 Use it to change your own morale and behaviour too.
6 Complete other points as they relate to you, according to your needs.

Create your answers

● Of the above ideas, which one is likely to yield the best results for you?
● What percentage performance increase could you realistically expect?
● How long would it take:
   – to develop the idea
   – to get results?
● Who would have to be involved?
● What date should you start?
● What is the first step you should take?

Actions I will take

Skills building	
Progress	
Reinforcement stages	1
	2
	3
	4
	5
Morale and behaviour	

Summary

Today you learned about an intriguing method of training, developed for dolphins, and its adaptability to raising human performance. We looked at its application to students, employees, yourself and others.

You saw examples of stages of reinforcement that you can use when working on performance improvement in the work arena and personal arena. You saw how important it is to provide the right increment of reinforcement, how to stabilize it and then move on to the next target level of performance.

When applying the dolphin method to yourself, we looked at the importance of being your own coach, setting the desired achievement levels and preparing for every stage before starting stage one.

I also showed you the way I personally used the system to train trainers in my own organization, and the comment of one of our training centre managers who saw people changing in front of his own eyes, while hardly believing it could be possible. I urge you to try it – the results can be miraculous! Here's a tip to get you started: success begins with the right planning of increments in small steps with multiple reinforcements.

SUNDAY MONDAY TUESDAY WEDNESDAY THURSDAY FRIDAY SATURDAY

Fact-check (answers at the back)

1. The dolphin process can work in raising the performance level of which groups?
   a) Your employees ❏
   b) Your family ❏
   c) Your local sports team ❏
   d) All of the above ❏

2. In training dolphins to jump higher, what does the trainer do when the dolphin jumps to its highest current level?
   a) Pats its head ❏
   b) Blows a whistle ❏
   c) Claps ❏
   d) Flashes a light ❏

3. When the dolphin stabilizes at that level, what does the trainer do?
   a) Raises the level at which the whistle is blown ❏
   b) Lowers the level ❏
   c) Flashes two lights ❏
   d) Stops the training for that day ❏

4. Whose performance can the dolphin process be used to improve?
   a) Employees' ❏
   b) Students' ❏
   c) Yours and almost anyone's ❏
   d) All of the above ❏

5. How many stages did it take to improve the performance of the employee who needed to communicate his ideas at meetings?
   a) Two ❏
   b) Four ❏
   c) Six ❏
   d) Eight ❏

6. In using the process, when is the best time to give reinforcement?
   a) In private ❏
   b) Instantly, even with others around ❏
   c) After work ❏
   d) During performance reviews ❏

7. For each stage of the process, what should you do?
   a) Plan your reinforcement levels ahead of time ❏
   b) Stick with the reinforcement of each stage until you are confident it is stabilized ❏
   c) Be patient ❏
   d) All of the above ❏

8. What can happen if you choose too few stages of reinforcement?
   a) Chaos ❏
   b) Less success than desired ❏
   c) Demotivation ❏
   d) All of the above ❏

9. What does setting the level correctly for each increment of reinforcement depend on?
   a) Making each level achievable according to each person's skill level ❏
   b) How fast you want results ❏
   c) Making each level achievable according to the needs of the organization ❏
   d) None of the above ❏

10. What should you do when applying the process to your own situation?

a) Decide what performance or achievement level you would like to reach ❏

b) Be your own coach ❏

c) Make a list and get everything ready for every stage before you start ❏

d) All of the above ❏

SUNDAY

MONDAY

TUESDAY

WEDNESDAY

THURSDAY

FRIDAY

SATURDAY

FRIDAY

Stamp out procrastination

Even if you've never been a procrastinator yourself, the chances are you know someone who is. Other people procrastinating – whether it's a work colleague, child or spouse – can drive you crazy and limit their achievement. If that's your case, or if you know that you yourself procrastinate more than you'd like to, you'll find that what you'll learn today will effectively help you succeed in stamping out procrastination.

Being a non-procrastinator myself, I wanted to find out why people procrastinate, why they put themselves under such stress and cause themselves such agony. In interviewing procrastinators, I discovered a great deal about streamlining my own processes to become more effective. As in all things in life, if you can understand it from the inside out, and if you can segment it and label each part, your ability to deal with it improves tenfold.

In my research top performers all tell me, 'Anybody can do it, Christine.' That may be true, but we need to know *what* to do in order to do it! That's what you'll discover today, so enjoy learning all the great tips, such as:

- make it look routine
- sweep away all unknowns
- press the starter button.

Procrastination syndrome

Let's look at a typical procrastination syndrome. Ron had a report to write which was hanging over his head. He didn't know why, but he couldn't seem to get started. He blamed it on lack of motivation.

The root cause of all procrastination is the mind's belief that the job is too big or too demanding to start it now. The mind prefers us to do routine tasks – tasks we are used to – because it can put us on automatic pilot to accomplish them. Then it can get on with what it loves most: daydreaming, fantasizing and reliving conversations or events of the past.

When the mind says that something is too demanding, what it really means is that it is **not routine.**

Make it look routine

When we try to engage in a new, non-routine task, the mind has to turn off the automatic pilot and give full attention to this new task. Since this distracts it from its favourite pastimes, it sends us messages that encourage us to procrastinate, such as:

- 'It's too much bother.'
- 'That takes too long; you don't have time now.'
- 'Do it tomorrow when you feel up to it.'

We have to entice the mind into participating, and the best way of doing this is to show it that the new task won't be so bad. The closer we can make it seem to its old patterns of operation, the more readily it will accept it.

The most effective way to do this is to break the job up into small, distinct segments. The mind won't object to tackling a small, familiar piece. It can do that in automatic. The smaller we make the pieces so that it can operate in automatic, the better it likes it. Therefore we create more chance of starting and finishing.

Sweep away unknowns

What if a segment has unknowns, you might ask. This is an important question because the mind will want to avoid unknowns at all costs.

What if we don't know how to tackle a segment? What if the facts are missing?

Let's look at a typical example. We have a task, we've divided it into pieces, and we discover one unknown against which our mind is likely to rebel. That unknown is 'lack of financial information'.

Get all the facts

We look for possible sources of information, put them into a list and plan to tackle them one by one. Our list looks like this:

- Ask experts
- Read about it
- Ask friends

But the mind's not very happy about that either, because it's not clear who the experts are or where we should go to read about it.

So we segment it again by thinking of possible 'who and where' options. This time it likes most of the results because there are few unknowns. It can be tackled in automatic.

Ron made the following list for his report writing.

Experts	Read	Friends
● Call Joe, my accountant ● Call the man I met last week at the Chamber of Commerce	● Go to library on Cromwell Road ● Buy a magazine at the railway station	● Call Jane – she runs a business ● Call Andy – he has a good accountant

The mind looks at this but it's still not very happy with one item. It doesn't like the idea of the Chamber of Commerce man at all because it doesn't know where to find his phone number.

'You don't expect me to find the number,' the mind protests. 'No, no, of course not,' we answer. 'I'll get it for you.'

Press the starter button

And so we segment it even further.

Call Chamber of Commerce man:

● Look for card in briefcase.
● Look for card in card file.
● Ask Andy if he knows number.
● Abandon if three above fail.

This time the mind likes it because it can handle those three on automatic. There are no unknowns.

But if we were to stop here with our instructions to the mind, we would never get started. Why? Because the mind hasn't had its command on *when* to do it. Therefore we need to add dates and times and create a chart for it, as shown below.

Anti-procrastination formula

Goal: Write report		
A. Segments	B. Sub-segments	C. Action dates
Call Joe	Get his number	Tomorrow - Monday
	- Try briefcase	
	- Try card file	Now - Sunday
	- Ask Andy	
Call man Chamber		Mon 10 a.m.
Go Library		Mon Lunch
Buy Magazine		Mon RR Station
Call Jane		Tonight Sun
Call Andy		Tonight Sun

Any goal needs segmenting. The major roadblock that leads to procrastination is lack of segmenting.

That was the situation Ron faced over his report writing. Once he segmented it, he saw clearly why he wasn't motivated to start. It's because there were missing pieces. Subconsciously these missing pieces caused him worry but, without identifying it, he couldn't turn the worry into constructive action.

Remember who is master

We sometimes forget that we are master of our own minds. To nudge the mind in a new direction, such as to undertake a new task, requires conscious effort from us. In other words, we have to tell it what to do or it will automatically do something else. The best way to get it to take action is through segmenting.

For the best success, segment into the smallest, most distinct pieces possible.

Try the process yourself using a blank chart like the one below to segment a task that you've been procrastinating over or which is particularly important to you. Complete it as follows.

1 Fill in every component part you can think of in the A column first.
2 Use the B column only if there are loose ends in the A column – if you don't have the phone number, the materials or the knowledge, for example.
3 After A and B are finished, decide on a schedule for C, keeping the time frame as short as possible but not overwhelming. Then transfer the actions to a diary or 'to do' list for each appropriate day.

You may want to make copies of the blank chart below for use on various projects in the future, and keep these to hand.

Anti-procrastination formula

Goal:		
A. Segments	B. Sub-segments	C. Action dates

People skills in action

Use an actions table like the one below to enhance your own techniques and achievements. Ideas for development include the following.

1 Stop procrastination by making the job seem routine.
2 Sweep away unknowns: get all the facts.
3 Learn to eliminate the mind's excuses.
4 Press the starter button.
5 Complete other points as they relate to you, according to your needs.

Create your answers

- Of the above ideas, which one is likely to yield the best results for you?
- What percentage performance increase could you realistically expect?
- How long would it take:
  - to develop the idea
  - to get results?
- Who would have to be involved?
- What date should you start?
- What is the first step you should take?

Actions I will take

Make it look routine	
Sweep away unknowns: get all the facts	1 2 3 4
Press the starter button	

Summary

Today we looked at the root causes of procrastination and how to overcome them. Fascinating aspects of the mind's belief system were revealed as well as tricks of the trade for taking command.

We learned that, when the mind tells us that something is too demanding and that we should procrastinate, what it is really saying is that the task is not routine enough to do while the mind is on autopilot.

We learned of the essential ways to segment any goal to make it more routine, to appeal to the mind, to sweep away the unknowns and to press the starter button.

We provided you with the all-important 'anti-procrastination formula' in chart form, which shows you at a glance how to segment your goals for success. Through the examples and methods, you'll have every chance of tackling even the most momentous of procrastinated projects, including those that have been sitting on the sidelines year after year.

SUNDAY
MONDAY
TUESDAY
WEDNESDAY
THURSDAY
FRIDAY
SATURDAY

Fact-check (answers at the back)

1. What is the root cause of procrastination?
   a) Laziness ❑
   b) The mind's belief that the job is too big or too demanding to start now ❑
   c) Fear ❑
   d) The mind's belief that it is easier to forget about it ❑

2. When the mind says that a job is too demanding, what does it really mean?
   a) It's impossible ❑
   b) It's complicated ❑
   c) It's not routine ❑
   d) It's challenging ❑

3. To overcome procrastination, how can we entice the mind to participate?
   a) By showing it that the task will be good for us ❑
   b) By showing it that the task will be quite routine ❑
   c) By showing it that the task will make us feel good ❑
   d) By offering it a sense of accomplishment ❑

4. If we divide a task into small pieces, what can the mind do?
   a) Think each piece through ❑
   b) Rush on to the next piece ❑
   c) Operate on autopilot ❑
   d) Give us cues ❑

5. What does the mind want to avoid at all costs when it comes to procrastination?
   a) Failure ❑
   b) Rushing ❑
   c) Resting ❑
   d) Unknowns ❑

6. What does a good anti-procrastination formula have?
   a) Segments ❑
   b) Sub-segments ❑
   c) Action dates ❑
   d) All of the above ❑

7. What major roadblock leads to procrastination?
   a) Lack of scheduling ❑
   b) Lack of immediate action ❑
   c) Lack of motivation ❑
   d) Lack of segmenting ❑

8. What do we sometimes forget?
   a) What success means ❑
   b) Why we want something ❑
   c) That we are masters of our own mind ❑
   d) That procrastination is destructive ❑

9. What do we need when nudging the mind into undertaking a new task?
   a) Diligence ❑
   b) Motivation ❑
   c) Dedication ❑
   d) Conscious effort ❑

10. For best success, how should we divide our segments?
    a) Into the smallest, most distinct pieces possible ❑
    b) Into the smallest pieces possible ❑
    c) Into the biggest pieces possible ❑
    d) Into the most memorable pieces ❑

SATURDAY

Magnify goal setting – magnify success

One of the biggest challenges for business owners and managers, in any field, is keeping employees on track. Goals must be crystal clear and communicated with the same clarity to even the most reliable and talented staff members. The same is true in our personal lives – it's so easy to get distracted by the 'smorgasbord of life' and away from our goals.

One day I had an insight that changed my life. I invited a specialist to address my trainers and consultants during a management meeting. He asked us to consider the difference between urgent and important. He explained that often something seems urgent because we are being pressured by outsiders or by ourselves, but it's not at all important in relation to reaching our specified goals.

That one insight made me examine all my actions – not only as an employer, but in my personal life as well. I learned to streamline my activities and focus on only those leading to my goals. Without that insight, this book most likely would not be in your hands today. Nor would my other accomplishments have been likely.

Read on and see how it can change your life too!

Twenty-four hours in a day

It's true that there are only 24 hours in a day. Why is it then that some people seem to accomplish so much while others can't, no matter how hard they try? It's the same 24 hours for everyone.

When we focus time and energy in a specific direction, we achieve a lot. But because life is like a smorgasbord of possibilities, the danger is that we reach in this and that direction without focus, ending up with an interesting but not very productive hodge-podge of results.

Let's look at what blocks us.

Urgent versus important

Walter Blackburn, founder of the business trainers PeopleTrack, stresses the importance of realizing the difference between *important* and *urgent*.

We might be hounded by a potential supplier who tries to get us on the telephone four times in one day. On the fourth call, we start to feel the sense of urgency and that it must be important, and therefore we take the call. However, in terms of our priorities its importance is low.

Everyone's day is full of these urgencies and distractions. Yet the people who achieve the most do so because they focus on the steps that lead to their goal.

> *'On the day we die, no matter how hard we worked, we will still be thinking of things we could have done.'*
>
> Anon.

Since there is not enough time to do everything, we have to choose our path consciously, not be taken down it by default.

The choice is ours

Most people think the culprit in life is lack of time. In fact, the culprit is abdication of responsibility over making choices.

Watching television brings relaxation. That's a reward. For the same hour per day that we might devote to watching TV, which adds up to seven hours per week, we could write a book and have it finished in six months or learn to play tennis well. These are different rewards. The choice is ours.

It's important to come to terms with this. Some people, for example, tell me that they think I'm hard working. They look at the output and think it must have been hard work. But it's not. It's a matter of doing, in the same time, actions directly connected with priority goals rather than actions that divert and dilute the output.

Twenty actions connected to two goals further those goals more than 20 actions connected to 20 goals.

Here are three examples of what can happen.

Example 1

Ian has a reputation for being late to every meeting. His own perception of himself is that he's just on time. His behaviour is such that he catches planes with 30 seconds to spare; sometimes they hold the plane while he runs to the gate. His colleagues have stopped travelling with him and his wife is in despair. They can't stand the stress.

However, Ian's perception of himself is that he's very productive. With the vision that life is an endless choice of possibilities, let's follow Ian around his office prior to his important airport meeting with a customer and their flight together that leaves at 2 p.m.

It's 11 a.m. and he feels pretty good. The drive to the airport takes one hour if traffic is light. He looks at his watch; there's time for one more phone call. After the phone call he heads for the copier, sees a stack of files for tomorrow's meeting and stops to put them on a shelf.

On the way down the hall he passes Joe who is rarely in his office, and stops to discuss an upcoming proposal that has a deadline two weeks away.

He continues on his way to the copier, then heads quickly back to his office to collect his coat and briefcase. It's 12.30. His PA tells him that Mr Barnes is holding from Australia, and he takes the call so as not to be rude.

It is now 12.38. With one hour minimum to get to the airport, it will be 1.38. Then he needs time to park and run to the terminal. The preflight meeting is long past. He'll barely have time to check in. 'Oh, well,' he consoles himself, 'my customer will understand.' What pattern do you see?

Don't confuse opportunity with objective

Example 2

Larry is a neophyte salesman. He goes on a business trip with his boss who is an expert in selling. The boss says they must devote themselves to making phone calls to prospects from the hotel between appointments.

Larry is a great networker and he decides, without consulting his boss, to invite some local people he knows to the hotel to meet his boss and make a presentation about their product. This is a favour he's long promised them, and it's a wonderful opportunity while they are in town.

The friends duly arrive to do their presentation. Afterwards, Larry's boss tells him that he is shocked: he thinks Larry has lost his sense of purpose, which was to devote himself to gaining prospects. Secondly, the boss is surprised that Larry didn't recognize that this time with the boss was a rare opportunity to devote himself to learning sales techniques.

Don't settle for small rewards

Example 3

Laura is a business owner, very successful but under stress. She's attending a weekend conference and her intention is to spend as much time as possible with other conference delegates in order to relax and meet new people.

She has one hour between sessions to socialize but decides to nip upstairs to her room first to freshen up. She changes clothes, tidies her hair, tucks a few things back into her suitcase and sits down for a glass of water. She makes a quick call home, then decides to change her shoes for the next session.

She then returns downstairs and finds there are only 10 minutes left before the session is to start. She manages to talk to one or two people but is left feeling disappointed that there's not enough time left to socialize as she'd hoped. Yet those were her choices. She settled for small rewards.

Don't fog your main objective

What is the common thread in these three patterns of operation? The pattern we see is that too many possibilities can obscure the main objective.

Ian did everything that needed to be done, but without prioritizing. Larry was blinded by options and misguided by loyalties at inappropriate times. He was confusing opportunity with objective. Laura sacrificed her goal for small comforts with smaller rewards. They were all caught in the fog of options, without goal focus.

What other beliefs keep us in the fog? Many people fear that, if they focus on goals, they will miss out on the rest of 'life', or that they will lose their creativity and spontaneity.

What they overlook is that they can use their creativity and spontaneity on those specific actions which lead them to their goal, just as well as they can use them on anything else.

Take a rational look at goals

When setting goals, typical roadblocks can be:

- confusing important with urgent
- wanting to accomplish everything
- not defining the goal
- fear that we'll lose out on something better
- fear of loss of spontaneity and creativity.

Do any of these apply to you? Use the table below to rate yourself on a scale of 1 to 10 to see where you stand in each area. Give yourself a 10 if you never block yourself from your goal and a 1 if you often do.

Blocks to focus	Rating (1–10)
1 I never confuse important and urgent	
2 I never think I should be able to accomplish everything	
3 I always define my goal	
4 I never fear losing out on something better	
5 I never worry that I'll lose spontaneity if I am goal focused	
(Total out of 50)	

How did you score? Where can you improve?

Now we come to the point where we have a choice. Shall we leave the situation as it is or change it? What rewards could we expect from change? Would it be worth it? If so, look at the processes we've covered every day this week and decide which you'll use.

Area for improvement (select from the list of roadblocks above)	Process (choose from those from previous days)
1	
2	
3	
4	
5	

Take steps to do it now

The next step in the goal focus process is getting down to it. A client of mine had a plaque on her office wall reading:

'What you don't do today will take twice as long tomorrow – and three times as long next week.'

Anon.

'Doing it now' means taking action at a time when our motivation is highest and our mind remembers the segments of the task most clearly.

In our seminars accompanying *Your Pursuit of Profit*, my co-author Bill Sykes stresses the fact that most 'A' priorities take only eight minutes to complete. Research has proven that to be true.

Take away the agony

The irony of the situation is that all the time and energy we spend thinking of what we should have done is far greater than the time and energy it would take actually to do it.

If we 'do it now', the rewards look like this:

- less guilt and stress
- more time and energy
- rewarding sense of accomplishment and achievement
- increased self-esteem
- moved closer to our goals.

Go for magnified results

If we want to improve our people skills, for ourselves and others, we can do what Benjamin Franklin, the successful inventor and statesman, did. Each day of the week, he focused on a different area for improvement. Then he repeated the cycle.

You have seven processes in these chapters for seven days of the week. Why not use each day to glance at the process for improvement and take some step, large or small, towards achieving it?

A small step every day gives us enormous accumulated results. As one man said about his own life: 'I'm 36 now and it will take me four years to finish my degree while I continue working. But the way I see it is this. In four years I'll be 40 whether or not I have the degree.'